WHEN A CHILD HAS DIED

When a Child Has Died

Ways You Can Help a Bereaved Parent

BONNIE HUNT CONRAD

Fithian Press

SANTA BARBARA ❧ 1995

Book design and typography by Jim Cook

Published by Fithian Press
A Division of Daniel & Daniel, Publishers, Inc.
Post Office Box 1525
Santa Barbara, California 93102

LIBRARY OF CONGRESS CATALOGING IN PUBLICATION DATA
Conrad, Bonnie Hunt.
When a child has died : ways you can help a bereaved parent /
Bonnie Hunt Conrad.
p.   cm.
ISBN 1-56474-141-9
1. Bereavement – Psychological aspects. 2. Grief.
3. Children – Death – Psychological aspects. 4. Parent and child.
I. Title.
BF575.G7C66   1995
155.9'37'085 – dc20   95-7780
CIP REV.

To all who ask, "How can I help?"

❧

When a Child Has Died

❧

Author's Note

WHEN my teenage daughter was killed in 1983, I looked into the eyes of my family, friends and co-workers and saw concern, confusion and pain. Many of them said to me, "Please tell me how I can help. I will do anything you ask."

Even though I yearned to help people help me, I could not tell them what to do. I knew nothing about child-death grief except that it was a terrifying, complex and excruciatingly painful experience I first had to learn about myself.

While traveling through grief I realized that, although there were grief books and support groups to help me survive, I was ultimately responsible for my own recovery. I also realized, from the sadness I saw in the eyes of the people around me, that while I had the right to be angry because my child had died, I did not have the right to express my anger by lashing out at others or by withdrawing into a shell of bitterness.

These realizations proved to be invaluable. Throughout the years, no matter how often I cried, many people stuck by me. Their presence gave me the support I needed to recover.

Therefore, this book is dedicated to all who ask, "How can I help?"

It is also dedicated to the bereaved parents who enabled me to write this book by unlocking their hearts and describing the pain within.

❧

Introduction

CHILD-DEATH grief. What is it? How does it feel? How long does it last? How can I help? If you have a relative, friend, patient, neighbor or business associate experiencing child-death grief, you might be asking yourself these questions. You might also be feeling uncomfortable, anxious or afraid. Knowing you will soon encounter the grieving parent at the funeral home, a family gathering, the grocery store, in your office, across your backyard fence or in your workplace can evoke a feeling of dread. Child-death grief is agonizing and terrifying for bereaved parents, but it is painful and frightening for the non-bereaved as well.

No one likes to think about death, nor does anyone want to discuss it. When a child dies, the subject becomes even more taboo. All too often the bereaved parents and all who come in contact with them, both socially and professionally, withdraw into separate caves of silence. At first, silence seems to be a safe haven, but just the opposite is true.

Because I am a bereaved parent, I truly believe that everyone associated with the death of a child, or with that child's parents, is, to some extent, adversely affected. Relatives and friends come to mind immediately. Those who were close to the child find themselves caught between their own sadness and their desire to help the grieving parents.

The aunt of a deceased child states, "When my sister's son died, I wanted to share my personal grief with her. Throughout our lives, we had shared everything, but she was in such bad shape, I couldn't burden her more. So I attempted to work through my grief by taking care of my sister and her family."

"My best friend's daughter allegedly committed suicide," says another woman. "I was angry with the girl for taking her own life because suicide is a permanent solution to a temporary problem—one which prematurely ended the girl's life and almost ruined my friend's. I was sad and angry at the same time, and dealing with these conflicting emotions was hard."

Other persons who can be affected by the death of a child are the grieving parents' co-workers, medical and mental health professionals, funeral home staff, the clergy and the police if they are involved.

This adverse affect, unless it is disclosed and dealt with, can cause unnecessary upset and alter relationships. When the distress and pain of those surrounding the grieving parents is kept secret, or when the parents' devastating grief is ignored, it adds to the parents' anguish and increases their sense of being isolated from the "real" or "normal" world.

If you are associated with a bereaved parent in any way, this guide will:

— answer your questions about child-death grief,
— encourage you to acknowledge your discomfort,
— ease your discomfort,
— and teach you ways to give bereaved parents both the short- and long-term support and understanding they need.

When a
Child Has
Died

What Are the
Bereaved Parents Feeling?

W HEN a child dies, whether suddenly or after a
long illness, the grieving parents' pain can
hardly be described. Negative emotions swarm them like a
lethal cloud of killer bees. Inside the swarm, they are being
suffocated and stung unmercifully, and although the parents might long for death to end their agony, they are, in
reality, fighting to save their lives.

All parents, no matter how young or how old, fear the
death of their child. Adult children expect they will someday bury their parents, but it seems unnatural when the situation is reversed, and the parents bury their child. It has
been said this unnatural reversal is what causes parents so
much pain, but it is much more than that. Nothing in life
prepares parents for the death of their child, and when the

child dies, they are thrust into a situation which permanently alters their lives in a way so horrible their normal lives are temporarily erased from memory.

* Shock
In the beginning, bereaved parents are in pain, but they are also in shock. Shock is a protective, numbing emotion that enables the parents to perform the necessary tasks of arranging and attending the viewings, burial or memorial service.

Shock can also cause the parents to forget segments of events occurring during their first few days or weeks of grief.

A mother whose daughter died fifteen years ago says, "During the month following my daughter's death, I know that I walked, talked and functioned. But even now, I cannot recall most of what I did during that time. Perhaps this permanent memory loss is my mind's way of protecting me from events too terrible to remember completely."

* Terror
When grieving parents emerge from shock, they begin to feel terror. They cannot imagine life without their child. They wonder what their lives are now going to be like, and if they will be able to find ways to survive the savage blow dealt by their child's death.

This terror, so intense and never before experienced, traps them inside a dark maze of unreality. At times, the presence of familiar faces creates reality, and the parents see similarities between their old and new worlds which anchor them to life. At other times, they are so frightened that these familiar faces appear to be distorted. Dazed and bewildered, they hear familiar voices, but sometimes these voices sound warped or muffled.

For a while, the parents might not see you and the relationship you have with them as they once did, and they can misinterpret the words you are speaking to them. As recovery occurs, they will begin to see you and the world around them more clearly.

Bereaved parents face other terrors as well. They now know that their children can die; that this tragedy is not something that happens only to other parents. And they wait in dread for one of their other children or a niece, nephew, or grandchild to die also.

In addition, the parents can fear they are becoming mentally ill. All parents react differently to child-death grief. Some become severely lethargic while others develop irrational and excessive fears.

A mother explains, "For several months after our son died, my husband and I thought we were becoming insane because we were experiencing a wide range of emotions normally associated with mental illness. A feeling of meaninglessness was the most serious. We did not know that meaninglessness was a normal reaction to grief, so we classified our state of mind as severe depression. We knew severe depression was abnormal. How terrified we were. We had lost our child, and now we were losing ourselves to depression and phobic-like fears neither of us understood."

✽ *Denial*

Intellectually, bereaved parents know their child has died, but emotionally, they can't believe the horror of their situation.

A mother states, "For many nights after my daughter's

death, I denied her death by rushing into bed thinking that after sleep I would awaken from this nightmare to find her still alive. I would hug her soundly and, with her arms around me, share with her the terror which had filled my night. She would soothe away my fear, then laugh with me. And each night, after black hours of tears and dementia like mind wanderings, blessed sleep would come. But so did sunrise, and the nightmare lived on."

For several weeks, the parents might fantasize their child's death was a cruel hoax. "How can this be?" you ask. "I saw the child lying in the casket. I know the child is dead, and, therefore, the parents must know it too."

At this point, grieving parents want nothing more than to have their child back. And so, they might fool themselves into believing they buried someone else's child; that the wrong body was identified by the paramedics, the hospital or the morgue.

A father describes his denial fantasy this way. "I knew my son was unemployed and needed money. So, for several weeks after his death, I fantasized he had taken out an insurance policy I knew nothing about and staged his death to collect the money. Some friend of his must have died, and I buried the friend, not my son."

To the non-bereaved, such fantasies are so implausible they seem ludicrous, but to some bereaved parents, they can be very real and very necessary. Such wishful thinking can ease their anguish and allow them to function fairly normally for hours at a time.

Denying their child's death can add to the parents' feeling of going insane.

A mother remarks, "For me, denial was wishful thinking combined with pleading. Even after my daughter's funeral, I found myself praying, 'Please God, don't let her death be real!' Or, when clenched teeth caused my jaws to ache, I would realize I had been chanting covertly, 'Please, no! Please, no!' Whenever I saw a dress or pair of earrings my daughter would have liked, I promised to buy them for her if she promised to be alive again. I couldn't tell anyone I was secretly bargaining with my deceased daughter. They would have thought I was losing my mind."

Some parents, in their desperation to escape reality, can act as though nothing has happened. A father explains, "For ten years, I somehow managed to live life oblivious to the fact that my daughter had died. As unbelievable as it sounds, I totally blocked it out of my mind. Then, I don't know why, I became aware that she was dead, and I began to grieve. My family and friends couldn't understand what was happening to me. They thought I had recovered from my daughter's death years before."

When other grieving parents hear of such absolute and long-term denial, they begin to wonder if they are facing up to their own grief.

"When a friend told me this father's story, I began to doubt myself," states one mother. "Child-death grief is very confusing, and for a long time, I didn't know which end was up. Then, when I began to think I was moving through my grief at a slow but steady pace, I would remember this father and begin to fear that I might actually be blocking out reality just like he had done. I felt this way because one day I would think I had finally accepted my son's death, but the next I would find I was still denying his death by telling myself this couldn't have happened to me. It was a horrible feeling, and made me more confused and frightened than I already was."

❈ *Guilt*

Along with denial, bereaved parents sometimes conjure up imaginary guilt. The combination of denial and guilt causes them to feel they are strapped into the seat of a runaway roller coaster. One moment, denying their child's death can ease their pain, but during the next, guilt can intensify it. Usually, perhaps because guilt causes shame and denial causes fear, the parents are reluctant to reveal the inner turmoil caused by these negative emotions—even to other bereaved parents.

During the first months of grief, many parents can even blame themselves for their child's death. They are tortured by self-incrimination: "Our daughter was so young to be driving. We should not have bought her a car." Or, if the child died of an illness, "We should have tried harder to find a doctor who had the cure for our son's disease."

These imagined guilts are a normal part of grief. Some theorize the parents feel guilty because they are alive and their child is dead. Society dictates that parents nurture and protect their child. Unable to intervene, to prevent their child's death, they mourn having life while their child does not.

Parents and children lovingly participate in each other's lives. Bereaved parents also mourn the loss of that participation.

As one mother puts it, "I feel cheated and robbed. I still have thousands of hugs, kisses and words of wisdom to give my daughter. Now that she is gone, they remain painfully bottled up inside me."

❧ Anger

Most bereaved parents, although they might not show it and are reluctant to admit it, are angry.

A mother says, "When a family member or a friend invited me to a party or to go to the movies, I became enraged. I wanted to ask why they didn't know they were talking to a dead person. My child had died. My world had stopped. My life was shattered. In reality, I no longer had a life. I was unable to enjoy the smallest pleasure. My pain was too intense and overwhelming, and I couldn't understand why the people around me couldn't see this. Sometimes, however, I did go out, and although I didn't have fun, I was glad I had accepted the invitation because I had survived in a place where other people were joyous, and because it reminded me there was another world beyond my world of grief—a world I wanted to live in again."

In parental bereavement, an assortment of angers can plague the grieving simultaneously. They can be angry with their child for dying and with themselves for allowing the death to occur. They can be angry with youth who, despite taking drugs or committing crimes, continue to enjoy the gift of life, and with other parents whom they believe abuse or neglect their children.

They can be angry with the sun for rising or with their dog for wagging its tail. But most of all, as one parent explains, "I hated and was jealous of anyone who was not in pain and didn't have the sense to treasure their good fortune."

❧ *Resentfulness*

Grieving parents can also resent the normal lives the people around them are leading.

A recovering father states, "I became very resentful. How could anyone feel comfortable laughing in my presence? How could they talk about the mundane? How could they continue to live their lives, to plan a vacation, to make love with their husband or wife or to enjoy a well-prepared meal when my life was over. How could they knowingly be happy when I was so miserable? Now that my grief is subsiding, I understand that others had to live their lives normally. They could not possess my pain."

Resentment locks bereaved parents into a Catch-22 situation. They do not want to be excluded from the lives of their family and friends because, if they are, they will have lost more than their child. On the other hand, the parents' suffering is enhanced when they watch others living the same kind of undamaged life they once did.

Some parents, although they might never talk about it because they feel guilty, harbor other resentments. They can be resentful that they went into debt or spent their life's savings on doctors and hospitals only to have their child die anyway. And older parents, who had been looking forward to enjoying their retirement years, can be resentful that their adult child died leaving them burdened with both their grief and the responsibility of helping to rear their young grandchildren.

❧ *Helplessness*

Soon after the child's death, the bereaved parents' pain begins to build to an excruciating and possibly disabling level. Their self-confidence can be worn away by the constant chafing of knowing they were powerless to protect their child from death; that even their strong love, hard work and vigilance could not produce the necessary cure, or lift their child's depression, or prevent the fatal accident.

The world as they knew it has become alien and strange. Weakened and weighed down by grief, they struggle to function in this new world—a world they do not want. Unable to escape from this new world, they yearn for the past—the familiar, happy world they inhabited before the miscarriage or the still-birth or their child's illness or the accident, crime, or suicide which took their child's life.

For months, and sometimes for years, grieving parents are unable to control their emotions in a way considered to be normal for adults. A surge of pain and a flood of tears can occur at any time and in any place, leaving them feeling helpless, vulnerable and weak.

A newly bereaved father describes his lack of control by saying, "I often see young women I think are my daughter. Each time I realize it isn't her, no matter where I am at the time, I cry bitter tears of disappointment. I am embarrassed! Before my daughter died, I was able to suppress a feeling of anger or hurt until I could express it in private. Now I cry in public places."

Bereaved parents also fear the smallest of problems—a flat tire or a leaking water pipe—because having to expend the energy to arrange for the repair might be the straw that breaks them. It takes every bit of energy the parents have just to survive another day of grief. They fear they cannot cope with one more mishap or stress, no matter how minor.

❋ *Detachment and Loneliness*
A feeling of being detached from the real world can also

occur. The parents' reality is that their child is dead. Everything else happening in life seems fake. This detachment is displayed to the outside world as absent-mindedness. They are so saturated with their child's death, they have a hard time concentrating on what is going on around them and can be extremely forgetful.

Inwardly, the parents might be thinking the subject you are discussing with them is trivial. They have suffered what many mental health professionals consider to be life's ultimate tragedy. How can anything else in life have any importance?

Along with detachment comes loneliness. Even in a crowd of people, the bereaved parents are lonely. They are lonely for the company of their child.

* Meaninglessness

Guiding their child along life's rocky road gives parents a mission in life. When their child dies, especially an only child, that mission is cruelly aborted. In the future, the parents might discover a new mission, but until they do, their lives have little or no meaning.

A father whose only child died explains, "I didn't want to get out of bed in the morning. Inside, I was still a parent, but to the outside world, I was childless. Earning a salary now meant nothing to me because my son was no longer here to share with me the pastimes that salary bought and paid for. Why get out of bed in the morning only to face another day of pain and emptiness?"

* Physical Problems

Bereaved parents often display physical signs of their deep grief. They may overeat or refuse to eat at all. They might sleep too much or too little. They might turn to alcohol or prescription drugs, or fill every minute of their day with frantic, and often unproductive, activity.

Child-death grief can also be manifested in physical pain, and the parents might fear they are developing heart disease or a stomach ulcer.

When parents experience child-death grief, they are besieged by every negative emotion known to mankind. For a while, be it several months or several years, these negative emotions are so plentiful they push out most of the positive emotions the parents usually possess, emotions which keep them on an even keel and give them the will to live life to the fullest.

While in grief, their demeanors can change in a split second or fluctuate wildly like an out-of-control ping-pong ball. One minute they can be irritable and short-tempered or absent-minded, and the next they can be self-absorbed and reclusive. These rapid and frequent mood swings can be very frightening and cause considerable distress.

In brief, bereaved parents can become—for months or even years—incomprehensible, volatile strangers immersed in their grief and their need to build a new life in the bombed-out rubble of their old one. But with fortitude, and if encouraged gently and in a positive way to believe that parents can and *do* survive child-death grief, they will recover and once again begin to live happy, if altered, lives.

And you can help this happen.

❧

How Can I Help Now?

THERE are many valuable ways you can help grieving parents. But to understand why your help is so
important, you first need to try to understand their pain.

To do this, recall an upsetting emotion you have experienced. If you have gone through the death of your parent,
grandparent, sister, brother or even a beloved pet, you have
felt the anguish of grief. When one of your children vio-
lated their curfew, you were anxious and fearful until that
child sheepishly crept through the door. An argument with
your spouse, your lover or a close friend left you confused,
angry or depressed.

While working through child-death grief, bereaved parents experience these same painful feelings, but they are

intensified a thousand-fold. The help you offer can be more effective if you keep this in mind.

❋ *Visit the bereaved parents in their home*
When you learn that a child has died, do not suddenly become timid and shy! If you are a family member, or closely associated in any way with one or both of the grieving parents, square your shoulders, take a deep calming breath and knock at their door. If handled properly, your visit will not be intrusive, and you will not be in the way.

A mother explains, "Immediately after my son's death, I needed to be surrounded by people. Their presence gave me the will to live when I wanted only to die."

Because this is going to be a difficult and stressful visit for you to make, you might want to present the parents with food or a small gift. Although you *definitely* do not have to offer them anything but your concern and sympathy, you could be more comfortable beginning your visit by saying, "I just stopped by to give you this." And certain gifts can be very useful.

You can put together a healthy assortment of snacks or sandwiches for immediate consumption, or prepare a casserole in a "freezer to oven" container which can be stored and easily reheated by the bereaved parents during the first hard weeks of their grief.

"At our house," says a mother, "had it not been for the many dishes of prepared food brought by caring people, we would not have had meals. Neither my husband nor I had the energy to cook because coping with our shock and pain took every bit of strength we could muster."

Or you can give the parents disposable plates, napkins, cutlery and bathroom guest towels. Often, their house is crowded with relatives for several days and such items make housekeeping easier.

A visit to the bereaved parents' home, even though entering an environment steeped in turmoil and sadness is the last thing in the world you want to do, is extremely important. It demonstrates your willingness to be support- ive and lets the parents know they are loved and valuable. Later, when grief makes their lives seem meaningless, they will remember that many people visited, and this will help restore their sense of self-worth and confidence.

✳ *Put your arms around them*

It's tempting for the non-bereaved to avoid visiting the be- reaved parents by telling themselves they don't know what to say. But physical gestures of sympathy can sometimes be more comforting than words of sympathy.

"I was saved by the nurse friend who sat up with me through those first dark nights while I tried to sleep," states a mother. "I actually shook through those nights. My friend held my hand, but she didn't say much. She was like a silent guardian angel."

Gentle hands placed in the grieving parents' hands or a tender hug will demonstrate your support. The parents know you are uncomfortable and afraid, because they are too, and often they don't know what to say to you either. But they do know they need you by their side.

"Simply put," explains a father, "I just wanted someone to hold me."

"I felt the same way," says a mother. "For months after my daughter's death, a female co-worker would touch my shoulder or walk beside me with her arm entwined in mine whenever she saw me. She would ask, 'How are you doing?'

I would reply, 'A little better, thanks.' Because for those few moments, her touch did make me feel better. These brief encounters helped me very much."

Before talking with the bereaved parents, try to determine what it is they want to talk about. In the beginning, some parents do not want to discuss the circumstances surrounding their child's death, so you might consider saying to them, "If you want to talk about it, I am here to listen." And do not act surprised if they respond by talking about everyday subjects.

A mother states, "For the first day or two, I knew if I talked about my daughter's death I would be forced to face reality, and I wasn't ready to do that."

On the other hand, some grieving parents will talk non-stop about their child's death, while others will not want to talk with anyone about anything. If the parents choose to be silent, do not attempt to engage them in conversation. In order to recover, they *must* be allowed to begin the grieving process in their own time and in their own way.

✱ *Offer a helping hand*

A visit to the parents' home gives you the opportunity to offer help or to actually assume the responsibility of organizing a meal (perhaps in your own home) for the bereaved parents and those who want to spend time with them after the funeral. Providing food and drink can be a joint effort; if you ask others acquainted with the family to provide a main dish or a dessert, they will readily comply.

"When we returned home from our daughter's funeral," comments a mother, "our dining room table was loaded with food. I didn't know where it had come from, but I was thankful that someone had been so thoughtful."

The bereaved parents and other members of their family need your help in a variety of ways. However, before you offer your services, ask yourself what immediate help you would need if there was a death in your family. Would out-of-state relatives need transportation from the airport, and would they need a place to stay? Would clothing suitable for attending a funeral need to be cleaned and pressed? Would someone need to be driven to the barbershop? Would there be young children, elderly family members or even pets who require care?

Prior to your visit, compile a list of specific errands and chores that you can do for the parents. Other family members are usually busy helping the parents handle major tasks, and because they are also in shock, they sometimes overlook the minor ones.

* ***Roll up your sleeves and get to work***
Too soon, the parents will be spending long, hard hours at the funeral home. While there, dust is coating their furniture and their laundry is piling up, so you can volunteer to become a temporary housekeeper.

A mother whose son died suddenly says, "A friend took over routine tasks in our house such as meals, shopping and cleaning. She answered the phone for us and helped in many little ways. Her hard work took off some of the pressure and enabled us to conserve our strength for the necessary task of dealing with our grief."

A second mother adds, "While my daughter was still in shock trauma, my best friend went to our house and cleaned her room. Later, when she overheard me say I didn't want my daughter's room touched, she rushed back and messed it up again. It took my friend three years to confess her crime—*a crime of love.*"

❧ *Don't give unsolicited advice*

A young woman who was seven months pregnant when her toddler died was almost driven insane by an elderly aunt who continually told her what she should and should not do.

"My aunt kept telling me to sit down, to take a nap, to eat a piece of fruit, to drink a glass of milk rather than a cup of coffee," remarks the young mother. "I wasn't about to do anything which would jeopardize the life of my unborn child, and my aunt's constant nagging seemed to suggest that I was."

❧ *Express your sympathy*

Most non-bereaved, as they fearfully approach the bereaved parents' house or the funeral home, wonder what they should say to them. Perhaps the safest statement to make is, "I'm sorry." You are sorry that the parents' child has died, as you would be if any child died. You are also sorry that the parents are in pain. Watching your friends or relatives suffering in a way which cannot be alleviated by anything you say or do causes you pain, and many grieving parents realize this.

Mentally, some parents are asking, "Why did this happen to us?" If they ask you this question openly, don't struggle to come up with an answer. In reality, there is no answer.

A mother explains, "When I asked my closest friend, 'Why?' she burst into tears and wrapped me in her arms. I don't know how long we sobbed together, but her tears let me know she didn't know 'why' either, but that she was sorry I had become a bereaved mother."

Bereaved parents want to hear that their child was kind or good or made a worthwhile contribution to the lives of others. When the child is praised, the dead hearts of the grieving parents are warmed and will eventually be brought back to life.

A mother states, "A woman friend told me my son was very special, and that he would be missed by many people. Her words comforted me because it made me feel like my son was important to someone other than his family. And several people told me that my son was a good listener, and that he had helped them with their problems. This helped me because it made me feel that my son cared more for others than he did for himself."

A father whose daughter has been dead for twenty years relates a similar story. "During one of the viewings, a male acquaintance walked up to me and told me that my daughter was the most beautiful young woman he had ever known. Then he turned and walked away. It was the best thing he could have said. His words still comfort me because, to me, my daughter will always be beautiful."

If you are a bereaved parent, you can tell the grieving parents that you know how they feel and that you understand. If you are not, do not attempt to empathize with them in this way because you truly do not understand their agony unless you, too, have experienced child-death grief.

One female visitor told a grieving mother that she knew just how the mother was feeling because she had an eighteen year old of her own.

"Her eighteen year old was alive and my sixteen year old was dead," says the bereaved mother. "I wanted to stomp on the woman's foot, kick her in the ankle and punch her in the stomach, but I responded stupidly by saying that having teenagers can be difficult. Three or four years later I realized the woman hadn't meant to be cruel. She just didn't know what else to say."

A bereaved father was deeply hurt when a female neighbor told him that God had taken his son because He wanted a special person.

"If that's how God works, I don't want to know Him anymore," comments the father. "Only a selfish God would take my son for His own pleasure. My God does not purposely inflict such devastating pain on a parent, one of His creations, and if my neighbor's God does, I feel sorry for her."

Some parents, however, are comforted by believing their child's death was God's will. "Although I was in terrible pain," remarks a mother, "I was grateful that my daughter was in heaven, and that God had saved her from additional suffering."

Considering these totally different reactions, it is wise not to discuss God unless the bereaved parents do so first.

You don't want to tell the parents they were fortunate to have had their child for *x* number of years.

A mother explains, "When it is your child, one, fourteen, thirty, or even sixty years is never enough!"

Don't inform the parents of multiple children that their grief will be made easier because they have other children to love; don't tell the parents of a still-born child that they are still young and can have other children.

All children are uniquely individual, as are the relationships their parents share with them. The parents' love for each of their children occupies a special place in their hearts. Love for the other children the parents have now, or will have in the future, will not make them forget the love they have for their deceased child, nor can it help ease the excruciating pain they are feeling. The grieving parents might appreciate their living children more, but they will not love their dead child less.

In the years to come, bereaved parents will learn that time does not completely heal the wound made by their child's death, so do not tell them it will.

"Friends and relatives who were especially supportive," states a mother, "never told me that I would get over my son's death, because they realized the death of a child is not something you get over like the mumps or chicken pox. We make adjustments in our lives and eventually we recover, but we never get over missing our child."

A father advises, "Do not give us reasons for our child's death, or help us feel more guilty. A friend told me that my daughter would still be alive if she had been driving our big car rather than our small one. Years later, I still felt guilty because I hadn't made my daughter drive our big car the day she was killed by a drunk driver."

"And," his wife adds, "do not compare the death of a child to the death of a grandparent, aunt, uncle or even a parent. Burying the young person to whom you gave birth and nurtured and worried over, while in the womb or for the days or the years that child was alive, is a singular kind of hell."

Another mother speaks out angrily: "After my daughter's funeral, a woman came up to me and said that she knew what I was going through because she had felt just as anguished when she buried her cat! For obvious reasons, I almost buried that woman right on the spot!"

You might be telling yourself that you could never be so insensitive to the needs of bereaved parents, and that you would never speak out so carelessly. But encountering grieving parents is always traumatic, and it is hard to predict what words will fall out of your mouth during an unguarded moment of an extremely stressful funeral home visit.

✹ Honor the memory of the deceased child

Before sending flowers to the funeral home, phone the funeral director and ask if flowers are appropriate. Many parents specify that monetary donations be made to a group or organization in lieu of flowers.

Other types of tributes can also be sent including those of a religious nature such as Mass cards, or shrubs and trees which can be planted in the parents' yard as a living reminder of their deceased child.

One mother was pleased when a friend made a donation of time and money to the group home for mentally and physically disabled children at which her daughter had been a volunteer.

"Although my daughter is dead," says the mother, "she is still helping those children, whom she dearly loved, through my friend. I can't recall who sent flowers to the funeral home, but I will always remember my friend's special tribute."

✹ Do not avoid the bereaved parents

Because bereaved parents—even the parents of the same child—grieve differently, associating with them on either a personal or professional level can be as unnerving as playing Russian roulette. You cannot predetermine their behavior by prior experiences you have had with others in grief, including other bereaved parents. Due to these vast differences and your discomfort you might choose, in the days, weeks and months after the funeral, to avoid the parents, but temporary avoidance can inadvertently become permanent avoidance.

"Many friends promised to call and keep me busy," explains a mother, "but they haven't called in four years! One friend that I had known since I was seven years old vanished from my life completely. I suffered two losses— the loss of my child, and the loss of my friend."

When you avoid the parents because you are uncomfortable being around them, your discomfort unintentionally becomes part of their pain. Their world has changed, and, if you avoid them, it changes even more. Some grief counselors voice the opinion that bereaved parents are partly responsible for maintaining contact with family and friends. To an extent, many grieving parents agree with this theory but add that making contact with other people is easier for them if those people have contacted them first.

"Having a dead child is not catching," comments a mother. "Other parents we had known for years stopped asking us to dinner or out to a movie. We sat here waiting, and we began to feel that our son's death was catching. Old friends would see us, turn and go the other way. It seemed like people were really afraid of us."

Although they might not want to admit it, some non-bereaved parents *are* afraid of bereaved parents; they are a living reminder that their child could die also. This fear is valid and understandable and hopefully will be acknowledged as such by the grieving parents.

During the months after the child's funeral, many non-bereaved are also afraid of how the parents will respond in a public place if asked, "How are you doing?" Will the parents cry? Will they not be able to speak at all?

Grieving parents are also afraid. They do not know how they are going to react to you because life did not prepare them to be bereaved parents any more than it prepared you to give comfort and support in this most devastating of situations.

✲ *After the funeral, continue to help*

As bereaved parents emerge from shock, the emotions of terror, denial, anger and imagined guilt settle in. When combined with the parents' crushing pain, these negative feelings create a heavy burden, and the parents have little strength and energy available to carry on the functions of day-to-day life. During this difficult period of the grief process, the non-bereaved can be very helpful.

Several parents state that friends and relatives drove them wherever they needed to go.

One makes the comment, "A group of people took turns driving me to the grocery store and to visit my son's grave. They also helped with household chores or whatever else needed to be done."

Very often, well-meaning people will tell the bereaved parents to give them a call if they need anything.

"We didn't have the energy to call anyone," explains one parent, "nor did we have the presence of mind to delegate jobs. We were too hurt and confused. People need to be specific. They need to state they will be at the bereaved parents' house at 9 A.M. for a grocery shopping list, or at 2 P.M. to cut the grass, or at 5 P.M. to cook supper. A time or two, when my husband and I were having a very bad day, we did turn away offers of help rather rudely, but most people understood that we were not being rude on purpose and continued to call us in spite of our prickly dispositions."

In this day and age, people are very busy maintaining their own lives. Reasoning that their free time is limited, they delay phoning or visiting the bereaved parents. If you believe that you cannot shoulder the burden of offering help and support to the parents by yourself, you can organize a network of willing relatives, friends, co-workers or church members to share the load.

A grateful father says, "During the first year of our grief, not a week went by that someone didn't phone or visit. It was as if our family and friends had formed a secret network to support us, to catch us before we fell into a black hole of despair from which we might not have returned."

If you live out of town, or the crush of responsibilities in your own life makes it impossible for you to contact the parents in person, you can offer sympathy and support during their grief by writing them letters or sending them a "thinking of you" card once a month. Noting these dates on your calendar or in your daily planner immediately after the child's death will help you remember to do this.

✻ *When the going gets rough, don't walk away*

When offering support to parents experiencing child-death grief, you sometimes need a thick skin and a forgiving nature.

A mother who has been bereaved for fifteen years explains, "A month after my neighbors' infant daughter died, my mother and I took several bags of groceries to their house. When we knocked at the door, the mother screamed that she didn't want to see anyone. We left the groceries on their porch and fled. Although my neighbors never apologized to us, they did eventually thank us for the groceries. I was fine with that, because I can still remember how nasty, angry and resentful I was after my own infant died."

Being supportive of bereaved parents is never easy. But if you are courageous and strong, and if you are willing to acknowledge their pain—and perhaps be the momentary target of their anger, or rejected temporarily—you can help save their lives.

How Can I Help in the Future?

THE most important fact you need to know is that the length of the grieving period varies widely from parent to parent and lasts for years rather than months, as is popularly thought.

When a child dies, and for the following few months or even a year or two, the bereaved parents are protected and cared for. After that, family and friends continue to be aware of the child's death, but they might not realize that the parents continue to grieve. For the rest of their lives, most parents will experience bouts of pain. This does not mean that some of them are not working hard enough to resolve their grief. These bouts of pain usually occur on family occasions; the parents wish their child was alive to share in the wedding of another son or daughter, the birth of a grandchild, their retirement from work, or their golden wedding anniversary.

Because bereaved parents continue to miss their child, the continued support of everyone associated with them—support which can be given in numerous ways—is vital to their recovery.

❧ *Share your knowledge and expertise*

During the first pain-muddled years of grief, some parents are required to handle complicated legal matters they have never handled before. These matters can include: settling their child's estate, dealing with insurance companies or, if the child's death was caused by someone's negligence or the child was killed in an accident caused by another person, taking legal action against that person.

If you are an accountant or a lawyer, offer your help. If you are not, but know dependable professionals in these fields, offer to schedule an appointment with that professional for the bereaved parents, and then accompany them to the meeting. These matters are usually private, so do not expect to sit in on the meeting unless the parents ask you to do so.

Some parents have lawyers and accountants whose services they use regularly. If you believe someone else has more experience in fulfilling the individualized needs of the bereaved parents, inform the parents, but do not insist they switch over.

In order to recover, grieving parents need to know the circumstances surrounding their child's death.

A father explains, "My wife and I knew every detail of our son's birth, and we wanted to know every detail of his death. We believed it was our right as parents."

If you are the doctor or nurse who was with the child when death occurred, or if you are the police officer who conducted an investigation or the medical examiner who performed the autopsy, be patient with the parents and answer their questions honestly and fully. You don't have to tell them their child was in excruciating pain or their child suffered horribly before death, but you can give them the facts.

Some parents, if they are not given all the details, waste precious energy trying to fill in the blanks. What they imagine can be more painful than what actually happened, and will produce more stress.

When bereaved parents suspect you are withholding information from them, they wonder why. Are you trying to protect them from some awful truth? Are they to blame for their child's death, or are you covering up the fact that it was your, or someone else's, fault?

You must remember that bereaved parents have a difficult time believing their child is dead. When they finally face reality, some begin to feel that life has cheated them. No one trusts a cheater, and the parents begin to distrust life. It naturally follows they will also distrust you if they think you are not being completely open with them.

✖ *Give the parents something to look forward to*
Before recovery occurs, the grieving parents' lives seem bleak and empty. You can help alleviate this emptiness.

A bereaved mother of nine years states, "Since my son died, my best support has been a woman who remains loyal in every way. She and I sewed together all day every Wednesday for three years. It saved me. Something had happened in my psyche that made it impossible for me to complete things. This woman and I worked with our hands creating something, and for me, completing it was very significant. To complete a skirt down to the last detail saved my mind. Even now, when we sew together, I think how wonderful she is."

You don't need a special talent, nor do you need to share a common interest with the bereaved parents to provide a ray of light in their dark lives.

Says a father, "One of my co-workers took me to lunch every week on an assigned day for a year. When I was with him, I knew I could be myself. I didn't have to pretend I wasn't hurting, as I did with so many other people. His acceptance of my pain made my life more tolerable."

If you are willing to spend time learning to read the moods of the bereaved parents, you will know when they are ready to begin building new lives. When this occurs, you might want to introduce them to a new hobby or interest. This can be a pastime in which you, or you and your family, are already involved, or something new that you and the parents can learn about together.

Have several ideas in mind as they might not like the first, or even the second and third, idea you propose to them.

❧ *Help pack and dispose of the child's belongings*

Some parents will want to clear out their child's room in a matter of months, while others will not want to do it for several years. Disposing of their child's belongings is an extremely painful part of letting go. You can offer to help the bereaved parents, but do not expect them to act until they are ready. And, when that time comes, they need to decide how they want to do it.

"I could only bear to part with my son's things one piece at a time," explains a mother, "but one friend was very helpful in giving his clothing and toys away for me."

Another mother packed all of her deceased daughter's dolls into a big box and stored the box in the attic. She remarks, "Maybe, someday, I'll give the dolls to my granddaughter. If I have one, that is."

And some parents will save a few of their child's belongings to look at later. It's their way of promising themselves they will recover; that at some point in the future they will be able to handle these belongings and remember their child with pleasure rather than pain.

✽ *Talk about the child and share your memories*

Bereaved parents face many fears, and perhaps the most significant of these is that their child will be forgotten.

A mother whose son has been dead for four years comments, "I do not want anyone to forget that my son existed, and a few of my friends have not. They still talk about him, and they still cry with me and share special memories."

The deceased child will live in the memories of the parents for as long as the parents are alive.

Says one mother, "My family and friends mentioned my daughter frequently, and no one ever changed the subject when I mentioned her. This was very helpful. The first time I didn't cry when I talked about her, and that was nine years after her death, I knew I was finally recovering. Did I feel great that day!"

Another mother is not so fortunate. She explains, "My family never mentions my daughter—my love. It is as though a hole has opened up and swallowed her—not only in the earth, but also in our minds, life and conversation. When I mention my daughter, there is no answer except silence. How awful this is. How inhuman."

Some non-bereaved, when they speak of the deceased child and then see the bereaved parents cry, think they have caused the parents added pain. But just the opposite is true. They are not hurt or reminded of their grief if someone mentions their child. Instead, they are glad their child lives in the hearts of other people as well as in their own.

As time passes, the parents will talk less about the death, but will still want to share memories of their child with the people around them. They want to talk about events in the life of their dead child as much as they, or any normal parents, want to talk about events in the lives of their living children.

"I am helped," remarks a recently bereaved mother, "when people remember things my daughter did and talk about them with appreciation. In a year or two, when I am again capable of laughing, I hope they will remember the funny things she did. Laughter is a known healer. I need people to help me heal."

"If you are uneasy sharing memories of the child verbally, share your memories in a note to the parents," suggests a father. "We forget, or don't hear, most of what is said to us in the beginning of our grief, and a written note becomes a permanent reminder of those memories."

✻ *Accept the bereaved parents' fears*
Bereaved parents wonder if they are going to survive their child's death. The painful and frightening emotions they are experiencing can cause them to appear to be abnormal, but in the majority of cases, these abnormalities are nor-

mal expressions of grief, and it's helpful to the parents if friends and relatives accept this even if they do not understand.

It is not unusual for parents to create a permanent tribute to their child in their home. One couple placed a framed picture of their daughter on a table in their living room. Surrounding the picture were fresh flowers, which the couple replaced weekly, and beautiful candles.

A non-bereaved guest in the home was overheard saying, "They've erected a shrine to their daughter. They must still be obsessed with her death."

These bereaved parents were hurt that someone was accusing them of developing an obsession. "We are working to recover from our grief," states the mother. "Recovery means we will establish new lives, and that we will again be happy. But it does not mean we will ever forget our deceased daughter. She lives in our hearts and minds and souls. Looking at her picture every day and decorating the area around it is no more abnormal than kissing our living children before they go to bed every night and cleaning or re-decorating their bedrooms."

▪ *Place a remembrance on the child's grave*
Visiting their child's grave can be traumatic for the parents. One newly bereaved mother admits she seldom goes to the cemetery.

"When I'm there, I picture my daughter's body as it is now instead of how it was when she was alive. I'm trying to erase this picture from my mind, and someday I will. But, until I'm stronger, I have to stay away."

Some parents reveal that every time they stand at the grave, they are reminded they will never again hold their child. This repeated reminder is like being struck down over and over. When the grieving parents see that someone else has visited the grave, the blow is less painful.

"Sometimes when I visit the grave, flowers are there," says a mother. "How rich this makes me feel. Anonymous love eases my pain and makes it seem like the whole world cares. God too!"

Another mother has come to know more about her teenage daughter's friends from objects they leave on her grave.

She explains, "I have found flowers, an autographed softball, pictures, a ring, letters, poems, toy animals, ceramic figurines and other treasures. Each object tells me my daughter's friends are good and kind, and reminds me that my daughter was too. Their love surrounds her as it does me."

❋ Contact the parents on significant occasions

All too often, family and friends are reluctant to contact the bereaved parents on the anniversary of their child's death, and on the child's birthday. This is not done out of callousness or careless neglect, but because they are afraid they will stir up the parents' pain.

"For the past twelve years," comments a mother, "a week or so before my daughter's birthday and also the day she died, I start remembering the events of those two days. I am in pain. On the actual day, I continually glance at the phone willing it to ring, and I rush out to the mailbox the minute I see the mail carrier. I still want someone, anyone, to let me know they are thinking about my daughter, and are remembering she once lived."

Bereaved parents appreciate receiving phone calls and

cards on their own birthdays and on holidays. But during the first few years of their grief, it is not appropriate to send them standard greeting cards. For a long time, the parents are definitely not going to have a happy holiday, or a happy birthday or a happy wedding anniversary, because their child will not be sharing it with them. It is painful when the people around them seem to expect the parents to be as joyous on special occasions as they were before their child's death.

A short note telling the parents you want to acknowledge their special day but realize it will not be the same without their child is a beneficial way to offer continuing support.

* *Don't expect a quick recovery*

Watching parents grieve is very painful for everyone around them. Because they can do little to relieve the parents' anguish, some non-bereaved will attempt to rush the parents through the grieving process. Again, this is done not out of callousness but out of a genuine desire for the parents to be free of their pain, and to be happy again.

A grieving mother's suffering increased when her sister told her, "You must get over this. Why don't you do what I do and just remember little Mary fondly?"

Bereaved parents yearn for the day their memories are painless, but no magic wand of words can force this to happen quickly. For the duration of their lives, certain objects, situations and places will trigger thoughts of their dead child, and for part of that time, they will cry out in pain.

If you are supportive, you will cry with the bereaved parents or sit with them while they cry, but you will not tell them, as a family member actually told one mother, "I want you to shut up, quit your crying, and get on with your life."

* *Don't be judgmental*

No one, not even other bereaved parents, can tell grieving parents how or for how long they should grieve.

An essential part of the recovery process is what grieving parents call grief work. The type of grief work parents choose to do is unique to them, and should not be commented upon by others out of worry or fear.

"My grief work," explains a mother, "was simple. If I felt I could not endure the increased pain that participation in a certain event would cause, I did not participate. If I felt the event was going to cause only a small amount of increased pain, and that I needed to prove to myself I could survive that pain, I did participate. On occasion, my family was afraid I was withdrawing and was going to become a recluse. But when I told them what I was doing and why, they stopped worrying."

The death of a child can be the catalyst which pushes the parents off in a never-before-thought-of direction. If they choose to work through their grief by retiring early from their paying jobs to do volunteer work, or becoming active in a specific organization, or going off to explore the country on motorcycles or taking up tap dancing, try not to voice your apprehension. They would rather you praise their courage and their determination to recover.

Grief experts advise bereaved parents not to make major changes in their lives for at least one year after their child's death, but, according to one mother, this advice is not always valid.

She says, "My husband and I decided that we were the only experts on our grief. We were willing to listen to the opinions of others, but knew that final decisions had to be ours. Although family and friends talked against it, I quit my job three months after our child's death, and because we knew it was right for us, we sold our large home and moved to a smaller one. We have never regretted making these major decisions so quickly. The changes we made in our lives helped us move forward in our grief."

The parents can be cautioned not to make major changes in their lives recklessly, but only they can decide what they need to do to recover and when they need to do it.

✷ If necessary, guide the parents toward professional help
Seeking professional help for grieving parents who you suspect are getting worse rather than better does not necessarily mean rushing them off to see a therapist.

One bereaved mother, who truly believed she had become mentally ill because of her frequent mood swings and excessive fear for her living children, did visit a psychologist.

She states, "When I told him my child had died and described my feelings, he replied I was completely normal. 'You don't need a psychologist,' he said. 'You need to join a support group for bereaved parents. You need to be with people who have shared your experience and have felt the same way you feel.'"

A mother who is a member of a support group remarks, "I joined a support group because I needed a place where death could be discussed openly, and my grief shared with others. I knew my grief was normal but hardly anyone else did. When I wasn't myself within a few weeks, people said I wasn't normal. My support group acknowledged that parents whose child has died are forever changed, and that is as it should be."

If you are concerned about the grieving parents, phone a local support group (preferably one comprised solely of bereaved parents) and ask that the group's monthly newsletter be mailed to their home. Many newsletters contain the names and phone numbers of recovered parents experienced in talking with bereaved parents who are still struggling to recover. When the parents receive the newsletter, they will decide on their own if they want to phone one of the persons listed, or if they want to join the group. If they are reluctant to do either, they will benefit from reading the newsletter, which contains letters, poems and articles written by other bereaved parents.

Advising bereaved parents to read grief manuals can be tricky—even when the person giving the advice is another bereaved parent.

A mother explains, "While attending a support group meeting, I recommended to another mother a grief book which had helped me. The next time I saw her, she told me she hated the book. For some reason she wouldn't reveal, it had made her feel very guilty about her child's death. That was the first and last time I advised anyone to read a grief book!"

If you see that the parents are not taking care of themselves physically, or are developing harmful habits, you can suggest they see their doctor for a check-up. You can also encourage them to accompany you to an exercise class, or something similar. If they agree to join an activity, you can insist they have a physical examination first.

Although all grief behaviors are usually normal, you don't want to sit idly by if the parents display signs of crossing over into mental illness. If they talk about committing suicide, or are unable to function for a sustained period of time, or act out their grief in bizarre ways, you can ask them to seek professional help.

But before you do, phone a psychologist or psychiatrist experienced in counseling bereaved parents. Describe the bereaved parents' behavior and ask the counselor's advice.

In many cases, the grieving parents' marriage is ravaged by the child's death, and divorce seems imminent. Here again, you can ask the parents to seek professional help.

Talking the parents into seeing a medical or mental health professional, or a marriage counselor, might not be easy. But if you are close to them, and have been an astute observer of the ways in which they are dealing with their grief, you will know the best way to broach this subject with them.

* *Reintroduce the parents to life*

For many years after their child's death, the parents need gentle support. If this support is given consistently, family, friends and co-workers can help guide them back to life.

After the parents' need to talk about their child's death subsides, you can begin to introduce other topics into the conversation—newspaper headlines, novels, movies, sports or any subject of interest. In the beginning, such conversations might be difficult to maintain, but if you keep trying, the parents will eventually respond positively and begin to renew their interest in the world around them.

To reintroduce the bereaved parents to life, you don't have to be approximately the same age as they are.

A father comments, "Our daughter's friends, who were in their late teens and early twenties, took our grief in stride and were not afraid to cry with us. Eventually they became our friends. Now we attend their weddings, and they bring their children to visit us. We consider their friendship a legacy from our daughter. We lost her, but we gained the companionship of her friends and their families. And they frequently talk about her, which pleases us."

Bereaved parents, although their child's death changes them somewhat, are still basically the same people they always were. If you can overcome your discomfort and fear, and if you are willing to offer your support in the years ahead, your relationship with them will be better than it was before.

Along the way, if you occasionally say or do the wrong thing, don't chastise yourself. It is better to err while committing a *crime of love* than it is to *commit the crime of avoidance.*

Also by Bonnie Hunt Conrad

Who Will Sing to Me Now?
The True Story of a Young Woman's Mysterious Death
and Her Mother's Journey Through Grief

Published by Books Unlimited, Baltimore, Maryland
ISBN 1-883612-04-07
order from your local bookstore

When a Child Has Been Murdered
Ways You Can Help the Grieving Parents

Published by Baywood Publishing Company, Inc.
Amityville, New York
ISBN 0-89503-186-8
books can be ordered by calling 1-800-638-7819